Learn From the Generals of the Markets

Azeez Mustapha

ADVFN BOOKS

CONTENTS

INTRODUCTION

This book profiles twenty renowned super traders from around the world, great traders who know what it takes to be successful in the markets. For those who want to attain success by trial and error, it would take many years of harrowing experience to attain success. Nevertheless, for those who are guided by the principles adopted and revealed by the traders who are already victorious, the learning curve can be sped up and the journey made smoother. This means that it will take a far shorter period to attain success if you learn from the industry experts.

Some people do not want to hear this. Unfortunately, certain newcomers suffer because they think they do not need help. But trading is like any other profession; for example, you need to acquire the necessary skills to be an aeronautics engineer. Somebody needs to take you through the process. There are rules and principles to follow as a student of aeronautics engineering; otherwise you are headed for disaster. You cannot do that by trial and error.

Trading is no different.

You need to learn more from those who constantly make killings in this seriously challenging business. You do not need to dither. The conditions on the market will not be perfect: there will always be hurdles, obstructions and uncertainties. By reading this book, you will learn more about how to become better and better, more proficient and happier as a trader. You will attain peace of mind, knowing that you can survive in the markets, no matter what they throw at you.

CHAPTER 1

Julian Robertson:
The Father of Hedge Funds

"A Trader's worth is based on how well he dealt with losing trades." – *Paul Wallace*

Born on 25 June 1932, Julian Robertson is thought of as a father of hedge funds. He graduated from the University of North Carolina in 1955 and then served as a US naval officer, a position he held until the year 1957. After this, he worked for a stockbroking firm named Kidder, Peabody & Co. He eventually travelled to New Zealand. On his return, he started Tiger Fund Management, one of the earliest hedge funds. Between 1980 and 1990, he turned $400 million into $22 billion. But this was followed by serious drawdowns which made investors withdraw their money. Thus the fund was closed in the year

2000. In 1993 he had personal profits of more than $300 million. In the year 2003, he was worth more than $400 million. In the year 2011, he was worth up to $2.3 billion. He went short in some financial markets in the year 2008 and made about 150% on his two hundred million dollar portfolio.

It's noteworthy to say that after he closed Tiger Management in the year 2000, he kept on investing by funding and supporting new hedge funds. Now called an erstwhile funds manager (for he's retired), he still invests in the markets through his former workers who are now fund managers. These funds managers are doing well.

Julian Robertson is highly philanthropic in nature. He founded Robertson Scholars Program, a body which awards full scholarships to many students. He's also pledged a portion of his assets to charity (following the example of Bill Gates and Warren Buffet). He's an astute investor and a developer in New Zealand. As a result of this, he was knighted by the Government of New Zealand in 31 December 2009. In May 2010, the New York Stem Cell Foundation (which is a private body) made it public that Julian and his sweetheart (now late) gave them a gift of $27 million. In January 2012, Julian generously donated $1.25 million to fund Mitt Romney presidential race.

Lessons

What can you learn from Julian Robertson?

1. As his quote at the end of this article testifies, he made colossal profits from going short on weak instruments and going long on strong instruments. Clearly, this is trend following. So we can say that Julian Robertson is a trend follower. In the year 2008, in which many people lost their shirts, Julian thrived. In what some claimed to be one of the worst financial years, sane traders saw that the markets were trending downwards and went short or

smoothed their positions. Insane traders continued to buy in the context of downtrends or refused to close their losing trades. Can you see the difference? Follow the line of the least resistance!

2. Why did Tiger Management get liquidated in the year 2000? The reason why is because Julian suffered seemingly unbearable roll-downs (which could have been seriously mitigated by conservative position sizing and risk control techniques). Sometimes Julian bet too big, as revealed in the following quotes attributed to him: "Hear a [stock] story, analyse and buy aggressively if it feels right," and "When Robertson is convinced that he is right," a former Tiger executive notes, "Julian bets the farm." Betting too big isn't a good thing because it causes big losses when you're wrong, and this is bound to happen. Betting small leads only to small losses, which are very much more bearable and easy to recover when the market conditions become auspicious again. Whether you are a fundamental or technical expert or you combine both, what will save your accounts and your nerves is safe position sizing and risk control. If Julian had taken this seriously, Tiger Management wouldn't have been closed in 2000.

3. In spite of what happened to him in 2000, Julian didn't relent. He quit managing money for others, but he didn't quit trading and investing. This is a great lesson for us. Despite the fact that he's no longer managing funds actively, Julian still invests with the hedge funds he believes are doing well. Once a soldier; always a soldier. A true general of the market won't desist from trading altogether, even in retirement. It's a passion of a lifetime.

4. Julian Robertson became a champion, and has remained a champion to date. Certain traders become livid when they suffer huge roll-downs, saying: "That's enough! I can't continue like this." This isn't the best conclusion. The best conclusion is to learn from the errors that you made in the past, take invaluable

lessons from them and never repeat them. It isn't easy to be a champion as it requires great efforts, but to sustain being a champion is even more challenging. Being a champion isn't the end but the beginning of the story. After making several costly sacrifices to become a champion, more daily sacrifices will be required for you to remain a champion. One who's striking a rock will feel some formidable resistance. If you keep meeting with resistance while doing what you routinely do, search out better, easier and more productive alternatives. On his personal portfolios, Julian is still a champion.

5. As stated earlier, Julian Robertson has involved himself in humanitarian programs. He knows that he can't carry all his money down to his own grave. I believe you're on your way to financial freedom through trading and investing. Otherwise, reading an article like this doesn't make sense. Once you reach financial freedom, please don't forget the less privileged, the hopeless and the destitute. Reach out a helping hand to the needy. Put a smile on someone's face. Life is short. You aren't going to live forever, and when you've gone, people will remember you for whatever you did while alive.

Conclusion

One of the most challenging things in the art of speculation is using discretionary methodologies – for you make decisions based on certain conditions and experience. Being consistently profitable requires assiduous effort, self-control, sensible trading rules and perseverance.

The chapter concludes with a quote from Julian. It gives an insight into his core trading methodology:

"Our mandate is to find the 200 best companies in the world and invest in them, and find the 200 worst companies in the world and go short on them. If the 200 best don't do better than the 200 worst, you should probably be in another business."

CHAPTER 2

Sam Seiden:
Flying in the Face of
Conventional Trading Wisdom

Sam Seiden, a trading genius, started his trading career on the floor of the Chicago Mercantile Exchange. Since 1991, he's been involved in various types of financial markets. Currently, he's the Vice President of Education at Online Trading Academy. Local and international students now tap from his decades of trading experience. He's a fund manager and a Commodity Trading Advisor (CTA). He's a speaker to investment bodies, colleges and private trading conferences. He's authored Market Advisory letters. He also speaks at seminars and contributes to various trading magazines. By visiting

Tradingacademy.com, you'd be able to access his articles, courses presentations, and also benefit from coming ones.

Lessons

Great lessons can be learned from Sam Seiden, and sometimes, some of these lessons fly in the face of conventional trading wisdom.

1. Honestly speaking, most of the conventional trading ideas are rubbish. Why? This is because most of those who use them end up being unprofitable traders, even after having played the markets with those trading ideas constantly. Trading ideas that work are the ones that allow you to be consistently profitable. Our major aim is to make money constantly and earn a living from trading. Even novice traders make profits here and there, but they cannot retain the profits over a long period of time. How can you retain your profits?

2. There's someone on the other side of your trade who's trading against you. This person isn't your reliable broker, but your fellow trader. For every person that buys, someone else sells. When you buy EURUSD and it goes up and you're making money, all those who buy at the same time with you will make money. But those who sell at that time will be losing (reverse the logic for when you sell and the market goes down). That is the reality in trading. Trading is a zero sum game: whatever you gain comes from others who have lost their shirts in the markets, and vice versa. You don't need to see the people at the other side of your trade, but you need to be smarter than they are. For you to remain smarter than other traders, you'll obviously do what's contrary to what the majority of them do (the majority are losers). The human mind isn't wired to trade in an appropriate manner. The common human mindset doesn't want to trade in logical manners. Fortunately, what can be learned can also be unlearned. Through

your determined effort, you can condition your mind to trade properly.

3. The most crucial factor to consider when trading is the chart (plus the price action). On the chart, you can see where Smart Money is making long and short trades. On the chart, you'll see what novice traders might be doing. On the chart, you'll see potential reversal areas in the markets and capitalize on them with insane accuracy. These areas are called demand and supply levels. A supply level is where the novice would be happy to buy from the smart trader. This is where many enthusiastic bulls want to go long – to their ruin. The demand level is where the novice trader would be glad to sell to the smart trader. This where many optimistic bears would prefer to go short – to their own detriment. Neophytes buy at retail prices and sell at wholesale prices. One of the smartest things you can do as a speculator is to buy at a wholesale price (demand level) and sell at a retail price (supply level). This logic tallies with how successful retailers in the world make their money. It's just the same way with trading: except the market speculators do that in their living rooms.

4. Sam's experience on the floor of Chicago Mercantile Exchange (CME) has given him a deep insight into the market. The reality of how the market works has to do with the ongoing supply and demand relationship, whether the market is in an equilibrium zone or in a trending mode. Trading opportunities emerge whenever demand and supply are out of balance. Any type of financial markets and indicators will do only if you use them according to how the markets really work. Now, using indicators to analyse this kind of scenario is possible, provided the indicators are used logically (otherwise indicators would be worthless). These indicators can also be used to understand why the markets move and how they do that.

5. The best thing to do on the market is to buy when prices are on sale in the context of an uptrend. You'd do well to disregard any 'buy' signal when oscillators are overbought in a bullish mode. The best thing to do on the market is to sell when prices rally in the context of a downtrend. You'd do yourself a favour by disregarding any 'sell' signal when oscillators are oversold in a downtrend. Summary: Buy low in an uptrend. Sell high in a downtrend. And do it right.

6. There's no perfect trading system and there won't be one. Even the best trading idea in the world can't always win. There's no need for a perfect trading idea, otherwise the person would be the richest person in the world. Using logical speculative principles is the only way to stack the odds of success in your favour. Although Las Vegas can't always win, they do well ultimately because they know they can't always win. They simply follow the plans that make them smarter than others. This is how we get advantages over those who aren't as smart as us.

Conclusion

The sloth is remarkable for its stupidity; just as the novice trader is remarkable for making average losers that are much bigger than average winners. For you to make average winners that are much bigger than average losers, you need to learn how to be smarter than those at the other side of your trade. Instead of going for higher education for higher certificates in order to procure higher position and higher salary, simply build your trading skills and track records for increasing financial freedom.

This chapter concludes with a quote from Sam:

"Trading strategies that work don't change with time, markets, or changing market conditions."

CHAPTER 3

Louise Bedford:
Trading Secrets Can Be Yours

"After trading for this long I feel I should have some brutal stories, I don't! I guess I had great sources for learning and I always had a good grasp of risk management." – Chris Cashman

Louise Bedford is one of the best female traders on this planet. This notable Australian obtained degrees in Business and Psychology, and has proven to be able to survive all market conditions. When it comes to making complicated trading topics look as simple as ABC, she's superior. With her teaching skills and assiduous coaching endeavours, she's assisted many former trading novices to metamorphose into experts. She's presented some coaching works, including trading methodologies that can speed up one's learning curve. Even, many other trainers have followed her examples by using her models while training others. With great zeal, many people have been assisted to be the best traders they can be. As a result of this, she's a highly sought after guest speaker at trading seminars and conferences. She's authored some popular trading books such as: *Trading Secrets, Charting Secrets, The Secret of Candlestick Charting* and *The Secret of Writing Options.* You can benefit from Louise's excellent tutorial services by accessing her website at: Tradingsecrets.com.au.

Lessons

The most interesting thing about Louise Bedford is what you can learn from her example. Here are some of the lessons:

1. It's part of Louise's trading tactics to stay away from the markets that aren't sexy. Trading the markets that move protractedly in a zigzag or sideways or highly unpredictable manner can't improve your trading stats. Trade only sexy and attractive markets, i.e. the markets that are trending well (moving in a predictable manner).

2. There are highly successful traders who are also effective trading coaches, just like Dr. Van K, Tharp, Joe Ross, Steve Ward, Ken Long, Mike Baghdady... Louise Bedford, etc. These people have left indelible footprints in the world of trading (and they are still active). Learn from them; learn from other great coaches whose names aren't mentioned here. But you need to follow their track records first. I don't think people can give what they don't have. If a coach can't trade successfully on their own, can they teach others to trade successfully? I prefer to take lessons from those who are successful traders themselves. Are you facing recalcitrant challenges in trading today? Please enlist the help of a successful trader who's also gotten a nice teaching talent. I've done it and it's worked for me!

3. I'll continue to reiterate that our women have some precious innate qualities that can be used to their advantage in trading (but mentioning those qualities is beyond the scope of this article). Hetty Green, Linda Raschke, Kathleen Brooks, Kathy Lien, Tillie Allison, Dr. Janice Dorn, Louise, etc., are trading experts. Profitable trading isn't men's birth right only. Your girlfriend can be a successful trader. Your sister can be a successful trader. Your aunt can be a successful trader. Your niece can be a successful trader. Your mom can be a successful trader. Your daughter can be a successful trader. Your sister-in-law, mother-in-law or daughter-in-law can be a successful trader. Your half-sister or stepmother can be a successful trader.

4. What can you learn from trading coaches? You can receive peerless and insightful lessons from them, and these can take your trading experience to the next level. Louise Bedford, featured in this article, once included a helpful lesson in one of her past newsletters. Here's an excerpt: 'TRADERS – we're an impatient bunch. Some of us take our foot off the accelerator just before we cross the finish line. The lovely Verica Cvetkovik shared these words of wisdom on our exclusive Mentor Program forum: You take a little seed, plant it, water it, and fertilize it for a whole year, and nothing happens. The second year you water it and fertilize it and nothing happens. The third year you water it and fertilize it and nothing happens. How discouraging this becomes! The fourth year you water it and fertilize it, and nothing happens. This is very frustrating. The fifth year you continue to water and fertilize the seed and then... take note. Sometime during the fifth year, the Chinese bamboo tree spouts and grows 90 feet in 6 weeks.

Life is much akin to the growing process of the Chinese bamboo tree. It is often discouraging. We seemingly do things right, and nothing happens. But for those who do things right and are not discouraged and are persistent, things will happen. Finally we begin to receive the rewards.' (Source: Tradingsecrets.com.au). Did you know that someone who has planted a cacao tree will need to wait for four years before he/she begins to harvest? We shouldn't give up trading if we face initial challenges. Our breakthrough is nearer than we may imagine, and once we attain it, trading would become far easier. It's extremely difficult to achieve permanent victory in the markets if we aren't doggedly patient.

5. Everyone was born into this world with a potential for becoming a great trader. But as you expect, it's one thing to have the potential to be something, but it's entirely a different ball game to run in the race and actualize the potential. If you want to be a top trader, acquire a good trading skill. The market needs diligent, hardworking and skilled traders to tap its riches. You can't afford to trade the ways others are trading and become a successful trader. Others hold onto their negative trades and truncate their positive traders, but you can't afford to do that. Every potential market wizard would need to face severe situations, circumstances and experiences before becoming a market wizard. The one who will excel must be disciplined. You can be great. There's a crowd at the bottom, but too few at the top. There's plenty of room at the top, but the issue is whether you're willing to do the work that'll qualify you for the top. To remain on top, there's a need to continue to improve your skill and knowledge. Try to do things a bit differently from how you normally do them.

6. As unpleasant as losses are, for all traders, it'll take facing losses triumphantly to move you to the next level in trading. May the losses that come your way from now bring out the best trader in you. Are you facing some losses today? Congratulations! You'll come out being a victor. Losses are an assurance that there is something greater on the other side. It's your risk control tactics

that will show your probability of survival in the long term. It's foolishness to trade the markets without risk control measures.

Conclusion

Profitable traders face many of the challenges we encounter, and they overcome them successfully. Some of the sweetest moments of our trading life have been during the most difficult days. After all, we trade out of genuine love for it. Not only do we do the right things on the markets but we enjoy doing them and also get rewarded. Market wizards' trading ideas benefit not only themselves but anyone who learns from them.

This chapter concludes with a quote from Louise:

"You see, we live in an age of entitlement where the majority of people expect to win, and often give up at the first sign of a struggle. They seem to think that all they need to do is take that first step, and success will be assured... However, you and I know that this isn't the case. The first step, while hard to make, is simply that... it's just the first step. To really excel, you must continue to push forward."

CHAPTER 4

Philip Fisher:
An Exemplary Position Trader

"One of the great things about the market is that if you're a naturally inquisitive person, you'll never run out of opportunities to learn." – Brian Shannon

Philip Arthur Fisher lived from 8 September 1907 until 11 March 2004. After dropping out of Stanford Graduate School of Business, he worked as an analyst at the Anglo-London Bank, San Francisco. Then he had a short stint at a stock exchange office and later started his own fund management firm (Fisher & Co.) in 1931. He made uncommon and marvellous speculative profits for his investors. Philip was a very reserved soul; rarely granting audience to the press. He was also very choosy about those whose money he managed. But when his first book titled *Common Stocks and Uncommon Profits* was released in 1958, the book catapulted him to the ranks of the market wizards and a status of being one of the best traders of all time. Later, in 1975, he released another books titled *Conservative Investors Sleep Well*, and then *Developing an Investment Philosophy* in 1980. He was very good at conducting in-depth research on the companies he was interested in. He was a pioneer of growth investing and gained many great followers, including Warren Buffett.

Lessons

Here are some of the lessons you can learn from Philip:

1. Philip Arthur Fisher was a soldier of the financial markets. He was a market veteran with more than 70 years of experience. He died as a hero of the financial markets. Are you a soldier on the battlefield of the financial markets? Are you a successful soldier? Is trading your passion of a lifetime? If you didn't have this thought in mind, you'd better start cultivating it now. Trading is a wonderful experience and a fantastic way of life – something that will eventually bring you your desired financial freedom if you don't relent.

2. Philip was a very private man. Nevertheless, his trading and investing prowess eventually brought him into the limelight. You should concentrate on developing your trading skills; endeavouring to be the best trader you can be. Ultimately, your skills will make you a famous and a sought-after genius. You'll eventually join the ranks of the celebrated market wizards.

3. Philip was a position trader. A position trader is a trend follower who holds his trades for a long period of time. Do you have the patience and the discipline to open orders and hold them for as long as the trend is valid? As a Forex trader, if you'd sold the GBPCHF in July 2007 and held it till now, you'd have gained far more than 10,000 pips on that single trade. If you'd bought the

EURUSD at the beginning of the year 2001 and held it until the beginning of the year 2007, you'd have gained more than 7,300 pips on that trade alone. If you'd shorted the EURAUD from the beginning of 2009 and held till now, you'd have gained more than 7,000 pips as profits on the position. If EURZND had been sold (at the same time the EURAUD was sold) and held till now, you'd have gained far more than 9,000 pips on that. There are far bigger profits to be made by riding the primary trends for as long as they last, but, unfortunately, most of us don't have the patience and discipline to do this. Philip invested in good companies with highly encouraging facts and figures and he attained enviable goals in the markets (excellent profits). For example, he went long on Motorola in 1955 and he held onto that till he breathed his last (at the age of 96).

4. How did Philip select the stocks he would invest in? He gathered as much information as possible on a company. This technique was highly invaluable to him. According to him, there are 15 points to look for in a market, and some of them are quality management and good business characteristics, adaptability, conservative accountability, good personnel management and relations... great sales strategies, ongoing research and products development, encouraging returns, and so on. One thing that Fisher rarely did was to sell his stocks. He was a permabull: a style that's no longer suitable for today's markets. He once said that the best time to sell a stock was "almost never". On the contrary, I'd say that the best time to sell anything is when it's completely clear that the bullish trend has ended and the bearish trend has been fully confirmed (for position traders).

5. According to Philip, what you refuse to do in the markets is as crucial as what you elect to do. There are things you oughtn't to do as a trader/investor. For example, he said that you shouldn't overstress diversification and that you shouldn't follow the crowd.

6. I'd like to mention with interest, the title of his second book: *Conservative Investors Sleep Well*. It's possible to trade with peace of mind and sleep soundly when you have open positions in the markets. If I know that only 0.5% of my account is at stake, I'll be able to sleep well. But if about 40% of the account is at stake, I won't be able to sleep well. The same thing is true when only 5% of an account is being risked as compared to when about 75% of an account is being risked. That's one of the reasons why I recommend very small position sizing, coupled with other basic risk control tools.

Conclusion

Is anything standing in your way, hindering you from achieving success in the markets? Those who give up after encountering a challenge are feeble-hearted. Do you have a problem pulling out consistent profits from the markets? If the problem isn't identified, you might end up blaming the wrong person. Never let the fear of the unknown hinder the benefits you can derive from trading. The unknown has brought millions and billions of dollars in profits to many traders. That's why risk control is one of those things you must embrace in the markets. Nothing can give you confidence of safety and security in the midst of risk as much as conservative risk control.

A quote from Philip ends this chapter:

"The stock market is filled with individuals who know the price of everything, but the value of nothing."

CHAPTER 5

David Tepper:
A Master of the Market Uncertainties

"I try my best to look to the market itself for guidance. I believe that the market provides us with the clues we need to succeed and it is our job to be as objective as possible at deciphering that message." — Brian Shannon

David Alan Tepper was born on 11 September 1957. He's of Jewish ethnicity and an American. He went to Peabody High School in Pittsburgh's East Liberty neighbourhood. He then attended the University of Pittsburgh, where he got his BA in Economics (with honours). While at the university, he worked at a Library to help offset his tuition costs. After this, he joined the financial industry. He worked at a bank's treasury department as a credit strategist. Later, he went for an equivalent of an MBA at Carnegie Mellon University's business school. He was then employed at the treasury department of Republic Steel in Ohio. In 1984, he was hired by Keystone Mutual Funds (now part of Evergreen Funds). In 1985, he was hired by Goldman Sachs, and 6 months after, he became the chief trader on the high-yield desk at Goldman, working for 8 years. During this time, he specialized in bankruptcies and special situations. He left Goldman Sachs at the end of 1992, starting his own firm, Appaloosa Management, in early 1993.

In 2010, the New York Times declared that David's success in the markets has made him one of the most profitable funds managers on this planet. In that same year, he was named the 258th wealthiest individual on earth. As a profitable hedge fund manager, David is now worth $5.5 billion. He purchased an ultra-luxurious Hamptons mansion for $43.5 million from Joanne Dougherty, once the Senator, Governor and Mayor of New Jersey. The estate sits on more than 6 acres of oceanfront land, and David has torn down this mansion to rebuild it at twice its original size. One architect named Jaquelin Robertson is responsible for building the mansion to David's taste.

On 25 September 2009, he bought a portion of the Pittsburgh Steelers. In 2003, he pledged an amount of $55 million for the Graduate School of Industrial Administration – GSIA (now Carnegie Mellon University's business school). He also gave sizable gifts to the University of Pittsburgh, so that many of the University's academic and outreach programs could be well-funded. Another $3.4 million was promised to Rutgers University – Mason Gross School of the Arts (where his wife, Marlene, graduated). He's made other donations after this.

Lessons

Here are intriguing lessons from David Tepper:

1. Uncertainties have become our ally and helper. Risk is our auspicious companion. The unpredictability and the uncertainties in the markets have brought David an immense wealth (just as they've brought immense fortunes to many other traders). We don't fear the risk in the markets. On the contrary, it is the risk that makes us money. Without risk, there can't be profits. David took risks, even getting involved in the riskiest speculative decisions, and he's now very rich. What causes fear and stress for neophytes is what causes excitement and rewards for great traders.

2. You can make returns on your portfolios as you deal with the market uncertainty. David made 61% return in the year 2001 by focusing on distressed stocks (companies). Year after year, he made money by being greedy where others were fearful. He speculated on the markets that others didn't want to do anything with, and he made gains that others couldn't make. For example, he made a profit of $7 billion in the year 2009 by speculating on seemingly hopeless markets. No matter how big or how small your trading account is, you can make profits on it (although you shouldn't expect to make a living from an account that's too small, or else you'll turn yourself into a suicide trader).

3. David knows when to enter the markets and when to exit. As mentioned earlier, he likes to buy the markets that many people are afraid of, and he likes to exit those markets when people begin to develop confidence in them. He goes against the herd mentality. For example, in 2009, he bought the Bank of America common stock at 3 US dollar per share around February/March and gained huge returns when the stock bounced back and went north significantly. That year alone, he gained $4 billion as his personal profits from his speculative activities.

4. Any further information on David's investment strategy? He's an expert when it comes to speculating on distressed firms and debt investing. He invests in many countries and companies. He would buy companies that are close to bankruptcy, and then sell their debt as it matured or sell their stocks as they rallied. He also preferred to take risks on companies he believed could be bailed out by the government (so that they won't collapse). By doing this, he made huge fortunes. He invested in Conseco Inc. (which was near bankruptcy) and made 148% profits in 2003, as its stock recovered. In the year 2009 (the same year he invested in Bank of America) he bought AIG's debt for 10 cents per share and later sold it for 61 cents as the company began to recover.

5. David wasn't always right in his investment decisions, yet he was able to make profits that were far bigger than losses. He made some investment mistakes, but overall, he made more than he lost in his career. This is the real McCoy in positive expectancy and profit making. No matter who you are, your experience, education or trading strategies, you're going to be wrong often, and losses will often come. Nevertheless, the most important thing is to make more money than you lose. This is the secret of trading gurus and they know how to do this.

6. No matter the satisfaction and/or rewards you gain from your current career, you can gain more than that from trading. Trading is one of the best jobs in the world, if you can master it. Do you enjoy your current career? If yes, you may also need to think of your old age, when people will tell you that your services are no longer required. This is one of the biggest advantages of trading: it has no age of retirement unless you retire yourself willingly. Many traders today are former lawyers, engineers, accountants, doctors, and so on and so forth. Whether you're satisfied with your current job or not, trading remains a better option (please see the concluding remark on this chapter). Because David didn't really

find his office job at the bank the best thing in the world (or his last biggest opportunity), he left the bank and founded his own funds management firm – Appaloosa Management. This step is what has made him a multi-billionaire today, for his firm has become an ATM machine for him.

Conclusion

Your destiny in the market isn't where you are presently, so you can't afford to rest. The most tragic thing for a person is to quit whilst at the threshold of victory. It's good to enjoy success but far better is that such success remains permanent. There's nothing good about being an ex-champion!

This piece concludes with quotes from David:

1. *"This company looks cheap, that company looks cheap, but the overall economy could completely screw it up. The key is to wait. Sometimes the hardest thing to do is to do nothing."*

2. *"Those who keep their heads while others are panicking do well."*

CHAPTER 6

Paul Tudor Jones:
An Astute Market Forecaster

"Too many investors have no patience and discipline. These two personality traits are imperative for investment success." – Andrew Abraham

Born on 28 September 1954, Paul Tudor Jones is an astute market forecaster and a highly profitable trader. Paul obtained a degree in economics from University of Virginia in 1976, after which he began working on a trading floor (being a broker for E.F. Hutton). He was admitted to Harvard Business School and was ready to go, but he changed his mind abruptly because of a reason mentioned later in this article. Paul was employed and tutored by Eli Tullis, a commodity broker, from whom he learned valuable trading tips. In the year 1980, Paul started Tudor Investment Corporation, a firm that is now a major asset management firm headquartered in Greenwich, Connecticut.

Paul Tudor Jones would always be remembered for his accurate prediction of the bear market that occurred in the year 1987 (Black Monday). He'd gone short and trebled his funds on that crash. As a result of this, a video which features that unique prediction was made. The video is in great demand and expensive, because it's scarce. As of June 2007, Paul's hedge fund traded on $17.7 billion. The formal rule for the hedge funds industry is 2% management fee and 20% of the accumulated gains, but Paul charges 4% management fee and 23% of the accumulated gains. His net worth is roughly $3.4 billion, and he was thus named the 336th wealthiest person in the world (107th wealthiest in USA) in the year 2012. He's been involved in various philanthropic activities.

Lessons

Here are some of the lessons you can learn from Paul Tudor Jones:

1. You can't learn the secrets of successful trading at college/university. The principles that guarantee lasting success in the markets aren't what can be gotten through formal education. When Paul was admitted to Harvard Business School, he packed to go, but soon changed his mind. He thought the idea was useless, since the school wasn't going to teach him what he really needed as an aspiring trader. The real skill of trading isn't what is taught at a business school. The real trading skills can be gotten from your personal approach to the markets, profitable trading mentors with good teaching talent, and years of experience. There's no way around this fact. Paul's mentor was Eli Tullis.

2. Your success, if unusual, would make you a sought-after expert. Paul charges 4% management fees, whereas the industry standards specify 2%. Paul charges 23% performance fees, but the industry

standards specify 20%. Because of Paul's excellent track records, his clients bend to his conditions and wishes. You've got to try your best to be successful. If you do, people would be inclined to accept your terms and conditions. Otherwise, lack of success will force you to accept unfavourable terms and conditions, especially if you're desperate and have no choice.

3. Paul believes that the whole world is simply nothing more than a flow chart for capital. Because of this you should always be prepared to take advantage of great trading opportunities in the markets. These opportunities can cause swing movements in the markets – which are potential turning points at important price levels.

4. Being an effective market forecaster doesn't mean you'll always be right. Paul says: "Don't be a hero. Don't have an ego. Always question yourself and your ability. Don't ever feel that you're very good. The second you do, you're dead." By making a correct prediction, you're not an infallible trader. Likewise, by making a wrong prediction, you're not an ineffectual trader. Paul assumes each of his orders might go wrong (though he's an overall winner). When you see each trade as a potential loser, you'll not use excessively big position sizes, and you'll be quick to exit a loser at a predetermined exit point. People tend to risk a high percentage of their portfolios because they think a trade 'must' go in their direction. This idea doesn't pay.

5. Don't dwell too much on your past errors. Simply move ahead and think of the next trading opportunities that will soon come your way. Because of frigidity that arises from recent losing trades, many people can't take advantage of the next signals they see and thus lose the opportunities to make serious gains and recover some/all of their losses. Paul isn't disturbed by the mistakes he

made a few seconds ago, he's only concerned about the new trading opportunities that will come his way.

6. Paul likes to speculate around some bends in the end of market biases. While trend-following is a good trading approach, one should note where one major trend ends and where another begins. For strongly trending instruments, one would do well to look for confirmation of a change in the major outlook before one assumes the opposite direction.

7. You can increase your lot sizes when your account is increasing, but you need to decrease your lot sizes when the account is decreasing. This ensures that you make bigger profits during winning streaks and smaller losses during losing streaks. I've personally tried this approach: it works like magic. Paul says it's better to play great defence, not great offence. Use stops to limit losses (in whatever forms they come). Paul uses mental stops, and he's disciplined enough to respect them no matter what. You've got to smooth a negative order if it makes you increasingly uneasy. If you have some difficulty with self-discipline, then you can use physical stops and stick to them.

Conclusion

Many people desire trading breakthroughs but aren't prepared to apply the right trading principles. It isn't bad to start small, but it's bad to remain small. For you to be a top trader, you have to apply relevant trading principles.

This piece ends with a quote from Paul:

"Trading is very competitive and you have to be able to handle getting your butt kicked... At the end of the day, the most important thing is how good you are at risk control."

CHAPTER 7

Linda Raschke:
An Amazon of the Wall Street

"Trading is an ongoing education. But like all other forms of education, a tuition has to be paid. When you make money, that's great. When you start losing money, that's the tuition you pay to learn." – Peter Brandt

Linda Bradford Raschke (Commodity Trading Advisor) is the head of LBR Group Inc. and LBR Asset Management. This astute female trader has over 30 years of trading experience. A real amazon of the Wall Street, her career began in 1981 as a market maker in options. She first started at the Pacific Coast Stock Exchange and later joined the Philadelphia Stock Exchange. She uses multiple-timeframe analyses when trading, as well as speculating on several markets with several trading methodologies. Apart from being featured in *The New*

Market Wizards (by Jack Schwager), she co-authored a best-seller titled: *Street Smarts – High Probability Short Term Trading Strategies* (released in 1995); and the CNBC Financial reporter Sue Herera's *Women of the Street* mentioned her as an exemplary trader. Linda has been featured in many financial programs and media. She's also been useful for many acclaimed trading organizations, companies and conferences. During her over three decades of experience, she's taught in more than 22 countries. For more information about Linda, please go to www.lbrgroup.com.

Lessons

During her lectures and presentations, Linda has passed on many lessons that are surely of help to traders. Some of them are below:

1. Linda isn't tempted to betray her time-tested trading style, no matter what the markets are doing. You simply need to learn how the markets behave and how they work so that you can achieve excellent trading mastery. Market patterns repeat themselves, and once you've mastered these, you can develop trading strategies which would no longer require major amendment. If you have a consistently profitable trading strategy (an edge), then stick to it. Be faithful to your trading method, even when there's a period of roll-downs in the markets. Why? Trading strategies that work don't change with market types or changing market conditions, nor are they market-specific. Market behaviour tends to repeat itself and a winning streak is in the offing.

2. You've got to love stops like your Mom. Setting protective stops when trading should be as automatic as breathing to you. The stop is an effective protection for your nerves and your accounts, no matter what others say against it. Stops will one day save you from the markets that refuse to come back – in contrast to your usual expectation. Never trade without them. It's a foolish act to allow a

trade that could be closed with a negligible loss snowball into a huge negativity.

3. Linda uses different strategies to tackle the markets. There's no strategy that'll work in all market types. A trend-following system will fail in a continuously ranging market. A scalping strategy would go kaput in a strongly trending market, especially when caught in a wrong direction. A buy-and-hold strategy would be deadly in bear markets. The key to scaling through all these is to know the type of the market you're trading and the type of the strategy you can use for it, or you can use a strategy that works in most (but not all) market conditions. When you're frustrated with a trading methodology, that's when the markets are about to become favourable to it.

4. If you can trade with an edge, correct trading mindset and effective risk control tools, then consistent and permanent success is possible in the markets. Linda's LBR Group has been a registered CTA since 1992, and has remained active till today. Moreover, her fund performances have been constantly ranked among the top 20 out of 4500 for best 5 year performances by BarclaysHedge. If Linda can do this, other women ought to do it, provided they are ready to accept the truth about trading and move ahead. If a woman can achieve this, what are you men waiting for? Linda is a true amazon of the markets, just like Hetty Green and Louise Bedford.

5. The most important achievement you make as a trader isn't making profits – it is not losing your account. If you can be a breakeven trader, using that as your prime target, then it means you can recover any loss you'll inevitably sustain in your trading career. If you can keep your account safe, then you'll eventually make money in the markets. If you lose your account through excessively big position sizes, what would you use to harvest gains

in the markets when they start smiling at you? The best traders aren't those who make money during easy market conditions and then lose the money when the market conditions become challenging. The best traders are those who can survive all uncertainties and adverse conditions in the markets, and then make money when the markets begin to pour out their riches for lovers of trading. The most important skill is not the ability to predict the market accurately, but the ability to survive losing streaks and keep your account intact; that's risk control.

Conclusion

Don't force yourself to do what's contrary to the realities on the markets. Trade what you see, not what you want. As a trader, you've got to be objective and unbiased, rather than subjective and biased. Show respect for the markets.

This chapter concludes with a quote from Linda Raschke:

"Successful traders who have demonstrated longevity in this business have one thing in common: a consistent methodology with a demonstrable edge. You cannot trade profitably over the long run without an edge."

CHAPTER 8

John Paulson:
A Celebrated Gold Trader

"Work actively and constantly on turning a correct idea into a useful action which will then become an unconscious habit – if you do, you can manage to be a successful trader, too." – Norman Waltz

John Paulson was born on 14 December 1955, to Alfred G. and Jacqueline Paulson, who both immigrated to the US from different countries (Alfred came from Ecuador and Jacqueline came from Lithuania). He's the third of the four children born to the couple. Growing up in New York, and spending some of his time in Ecuador, he eventually received his first degree in finance from New York University Stern School of Business (then the New York University's College of Business and Public Administration). He was advised to apply to Harvard Business School and he was admitted. After this, he earned the Sidney J. Weinberg/Goldman Sachs scholarship, and at last, bagged his MBA in 1980 (being in the top 5% of his class).

Paul first served as a research analyst at Boston Consulting Group in 1980. He was very good at his job but he was not yet trading or investing. He quit that company to work at Odyssey Partners. He also had some work experience at Bear Stearns and Gruss Partners LP. With $2 million and one worker, he started Paulson & Co. (his own fund) in 1994, based in New York. This American hedge fund manager went short on subprime mortgages in 2007 and earned profits totalling $3.7 billion in the same year. In the year 2010, he earned a salary of almost $5 billion. The windfall was realized when the bubbles of mortgage backed securities market went burst. The bet against the subprime mortgage bubble was one of the best trades in human history. He's long invested his personal fortune in gold, and as a result of this, an additional $3.1 billion was made between the year 2010 and the year 2011. In the year 2012, with a net worth of $12.5 billion, Forbes ranked him 61st on the list of the richest individuals the world over. He's spent hundreds of millions of dollars in buying several homes. He's also spent hundreds of millions of dollars for various causes and charities.

Lessons

What can you learn from John Paulson?

1. It's common for many seemingly indigent people to be jealous, envious, livid and become forlorn when they read how seriously affluent some are. You're not really forlorn as you thought – only that you let great opportunities pass under your nose without capitalizing on them. There are many great opportunities in trading, but you don't want to be a trader because you know some

people are losing, and because those who are not interested in trading have told you not to do it. You see, they aren't doing it, and they are telling you not to do it (simply because they lack the knowledge that can really make them winners in the markets). Some people don't want to do it, while some do it in the face of recalcitrant hurdles and obstructions. When those who push ahead in spite of the challenges end up attaining financial freedom, then others would begin to be jealous, envious, livid, and would feel forlorn. Whereas those who have become rich as traders have done what you didn't want to do: they risked their heads, necks and shirts. Now they are rich, and you're furious and envious. When some Occupy Wall Street protesters were picketing his area, the angry John Paulson was reported as saying: "We pay a lot of taxes, especially living in New York... Most jurisdictions would want to have successful companies like ours located there. I'm sure if we wanted to go to Singapore, they'd roll out the red carpet to attract us... We choose to stay here and then, you know, get yelled at. I think that's misdirecting their anger at the wrong place." (An interview with Bloomberg BusinessWeek magazine, 2012).

2. Don't despise the days of your little beginning. Though your beginning may be small, your latter end shall greatly increase. John's beginning was very humble, yet he now has a place among the wealthiest hedge-fund managers in the world. Compared to what he's worth today, the $2 million he started with when he founded his own hedge fund pales into insignificance. Your background may be humble. What you have now may be very insignificant, but it's imperative that you concentrate on being the best trader you can be, then your latter end shall be increased greatly. Your potential in trading is limitless and can't be determined by the opinions of others.

3. John hasn't been always right, just like other successful traders. In the year 2011, he sustained some negativity when speculating on Bank of America and other business entities. In September 2011, it was reported that his portfolio was almost forty percent negative. Even recently, he announced about eighteen percent negativity. You see, these aren't the reasons for him to quit trading as certain people do. Ultimately, John would recover his negativity and move ahead; it's just a matter of time. No matter the trading system you use, you'll go through periods of winnings, roll-downs and flat performances. During these periods, you shouldn't feel discouraged or dejected; eventually you'll recover your losses and move ahead. Now and then, market wizards' performances are punctuated by periods of negativity, and there's no way around this. Ultimately, most of them (especially those who are good at risk management) would recover their losses and move ahead.

Conclusion

There were those who were passionate about trading, but today, everything has finally ebbed out. Don't give up! No matter how bad things are right now, no matter how hopeless your situation is; it doesn't matter how many people have told you to your face that you can't make it in trading. Things will turn your tide around.

This chapter concludes with a quote from John Paulson:

"Nothing is right in all markets at all times... Our goal is not to outperform all the time – that's not possible. We want to outperform over time."

CHAPTER 9

Jim Rogers:
The Nostradamus of the Markets

"Experience taught me that experts are wrong most of the time. The reason for my success in the financial markets is the fact that I see the world from another point of view." – Jim Rogers

James B. Rogers was born on 19 October 1942 in Baltimore, Maryland, USA, though he was raised in Demopolis, Alabama. He first experienced business at the tender age of five when he sold peanuts and empty bottles left by some sports fans. When he graduated in History from Yale University in 1964, he worked at Dominick & Dominick – a Wall Street firm. Then, he got his 2nd BA degree in Philosophy, Politics and Economics from Balliol College, Oxford University in the year 1966. He worked alongside George

Soros, starting from 1970, at an investment bank called Arnhold and S. Bleichroder. Together with George, he founded the Quantum Fund, whose portfolio was increased 42 times in ten years. This means they outperformed the S&P by more than 893 times. That Fund was really marvelous. He's currently the head of Rogers Holdings and Beeland Interests, Inc. and the creator of RICI (the Rogers International Commodities Index). That Index keeps tabs on the indices as one way to speculate in the index. Jim has always espoused trading agricultural products.

In 1980 Jim quit working at Quantum Fund and started a world tour on a bike. After this, he engaged in some interesting activities, but soon he embarked on another tour of the world, this time including China (1990-1992). This feat was a record one hundred and sixty thousand kilometres spanning six continents. As a result of this, he made the Guinness Book of World Records. Then from 1 January 1999 to 5 January 2002 he made another Guinness World Record by travelling through one hundred and sixteen countries in a custom-made Mercedes. He started in Iceland and ended up returning to New York after three years. More details about this can be found on Jimrogers.com.

He's written a number of best-selling books including *Investment Biker, Hot Commodities: How Anyone Can Invest Profitably in the World's Best Market, Adventure Capitalist* and *A Gift To My Children* (his latest book).

Lessons

What can we learn from Jim?

1. I call Jim Rogers the Nostradamus of the markets because of his trading approaches and style. He does what many traders wouldn't want to do, and he achieves extraordinary results and records that many can't achieve. When it comes to his perception of the markets, his views could be strange to many, but they are true. For

example, unlike what most speculators in the world think, Jim says the commodity market is the best market in the world. Do you believe this? How about other financial markets? The best answers are found in his book, *Hot Commodities: How Anyone Can Invest Profitably in the World's Best Market.*

2. What is the best city in the world to live in? Or to be precise, where is the best part of the world in which one can live as an investor? Jim is no longer living in the US, for he'd sold his mansion in New York and relocated to Singapore. He'd have settled in China or Hong Kong if it wasn't for the perceived high level of pollution in those countries. According to him, the UK was the best place to invest in the early 19th century, and the USA was the best place to invest in the early 20th century. Now there are economic power shifts, so the best place to invest in the early 21st century is Asia. Even certain small countries like Cambodia and Sri Lanka are fertile markets for investors (although he was pessimistic about the future of Indian economy, for he believes that India might not survive another 30 or 40 years). This means that the UK and the US are no longer the ideal places to invest. Apart from Jim, many assiduous investors and market analysts have often mentioned this fact.

3. Jim declares that Russia and the Commonwealth of Independent States (CIS region) have what it takes to be the leader in agricultural products. He said people should put less attention on stocks and focus on commodities and agriculture. He pointed out that rather than looking forward to Wall Street or the City professions, it pays to learn commodities, agriculture and mining. He was reputed as saying this: "The power is shifting again from the financial centres to the producers of real goods. The place to be is in commodities, raw materials, natural resources." In May 2012 he remarked during an interview with Forbes Magazine: "There's going to be a huge shift in American society, American

culture, in the places where one is going to get rich. The stock brokers are going to be driving taxis. The smart ones will learn to drive tractors so they can work for the smart farmers. The farmers are going to be driving Lamborghinis. I'm telling you. You should start Forbes Farming."

4. For those who idolize the English language, well this may not be the unwelcome fact. English language might not be the most important language in the world in the foreseeable future. The Chinese Mandarin is the language with the most speakers in the world (even the Chinese population is far higher than all the population of the 54 counties in Africa). The fact that I can speak English doesn't make me the greatest man in the world, nor does the fact that you can't speak English make you the most unfortunate man in the world. Perhaps some people (including me) idolized the English language because of the reasons that are beyond the scope of this article. Don't those who speak two or more languages have advantages over those who can only speak one language? Well, Jim's first daughter is being taught Mandarin so as to get her prepared for the future. Why? Jim revealed that the Chinese are highly enthusiastic, inspired and industrious; and that's the kind of environment in which one should be. That was how the USA and Europe used to be. Think of heavy machinery, electronics, goods and much more that are coming from Asia. More than half of all the robots in the world are in Asia. I was even amazed to learn that most of these robots help build ships and many other industrial goods with unbelievable speed. Are you prepared for the future? Do you prepare your children for the future?

5. With all these, Jim has always been, and remains, a successful trader. He knows where the best markets are and how to take advantage of them. This has really added to his expertise and

profile. Are you ready to take the challenge and trade your way to financial freedom?

Conclusion

Speculation has to do with taking advantage of opportunities that most others fail to see; and this is usually done before others see the opportunities. Unless in some obvious cases, the most common means to harness gains in the markets is when the price moves downwards after a short position is opened, or when the price moves upwards after a long position is opened.

This piece concludes with more quotes from Jim:

1. *"Do not buy the hype from Wall St. and the press that stocks always go up. There are long periods when stocks do nothing and other investments are better."*

2. *"Those who cannot adjust to change will be swept aside by it. Those who recognize change and react accordingly will benefit."*

CHAPTER 10

Mike Baghdady:
Price Is King

"Master price action and you will be well on your way to successful trading." –
Nick McDonald

Mike Baghdady is a highly experienced trader with far more than three decades of experience. He's been called Mr. Price Behaviour. He's a world leader when it comes to the mastery of price actions. He graduated from the American University at Cairo in Egypt. This expert, who was termed the World Live Trading Champion in 2009, was formerly an apprentice at a big investment bank in New York. In 1987, the American Chamber of Commerce magazine 'AmCham' awarded him the 'Trader of the Year.' He was also a physical grains trader in a commodity house, and has developed price behaviour rules that can be used to master many financial markets. As an instructor, he's advised major hedge funds and multi-national companies, including floor and private traders. More information on what he does and how you can benefit from his knowledge can be found at Trainingtraders.com.

Lessons

What does Mr. Price Behaviour have to say?

1. Yes, price is king. The most important indicator in any financial market is the price. It's the best tool to use in analysing the current situation in the market and what traders are now doing. When you study price behaviour and you master it, you'll have a deep insight into how the markets behave and how you can take an advantage of that. No matter the strategy you use, you would do well to use it in conjunction with price behaviour methodology and techniques. There are traders who are highly experienced as a result of their price behaviour mastery. Unfortunately, many coaches don't teach this.

2. A trending market would continue to trend until there is a factor that forces it to change its course. It's more likely for a market bias to continue than to reverse. The price doesn't move in a straight line. Oscillators which pinpoint overbought and oversold conditions may not be effective in strongly trending markets. That's why one would do well to stop trading against the trend simply because there are temporary reversals in the markets. It's better to take those reversals as the opportunities to enter the markets at better prices.

3. When there is some decrease in the momentum of a bias, it doesn't portend a change in that bias. It's only a transitory equilibrium phase prior to the continuation of the bias. A bias wouldn't just stop without showing some potential reversal

patterns, which are called chart patterns. It may take a long period of time before a confirmed bias changes.

4. It's professional to evaluate your speculative activities based on whether or not you follow your trading rules, without attaching too much importance on the outcome of each trade. The outcome of each trade is beyond your control, so what you always have in your control is making sure you execute your trades flawlessly. If that's the case, it would be easier for you to exit a trade at a predetermined market level, should the trade move against you. There would always be times when some trades are in the negative zone. This is what traders hate, and if you find yourself in this kind of undesirable situation, the best thing you can do is to close your trades quickly; otherwise, the more you run the loss trades, the greater the negativity.

5. According to Mike, the numbers of those who venture into the financial markets are increasing rapidly, while most of them don't know what it takes to be successful (they make many errors when trading). It takes a long time to become consistently successful in the markets. For some, the learning curve might be sped up (though it can't be bypassed). This means that some learn quickly and master the markets faster than others. While some adapt quickly and become pros in a few years, others would have to struggle with the markets for many years before they can become triumphant. One quicker way to trading mastery is to copy the techniques from successful traders. This can be your edge; even if you'd tweak the methodology to suit your personal needs.

6. You can read many books about trading, take many courses and go to many seminars, but it takes real practice and enduring patience to learn the art of trading. This can be done risk free on demo accounts (you see, online trading is arguably the only business where you can test your trading ideas on real market

conditions without risking your capital). As you gain more confidence and expertise, then you may go live and start growing your portfolio as you begin to mature as an expert.

Conclusion

All chart readers want to call trades with a high degree of accuracy. Since this may not be viable, the most logical thing to do is to look at what the price is saying and trade what one sees, coupled with good money management and effective risk control. So devising a trading methodology may be ineffectual without considering the unpredictable nature of the markets. Your analyses ought not to be based on certainties and blind courage, but on price realities.

One article from Mike appeared in TRADERS' September 2008 edition (www.traders-mag.com); the quotes below were taken from that article:

1. *"No-one knows where the next tick in price is going to be so the key to making money in trading is minimizing our risk and taking small losses. Try never to take big losses and always try to place the odds on your side. Profits will then take care of themselves."*

2. *"If you chose to use some technical indicators, they should be used as tools to confirm your trading decisions, rather than depending solely on them to initiate a trade. Simply taking trading signals off an indicator, or analyzing several indicators at the same time usually would have a negative effect on a trader's bottom line. It is very important that you're able to make a trading decision based on your observations of price action and what you see on the chart."*

CHAPTER 11

William Eckhardt:
The Oracle of Chicago

"If you want to get rich, just find someone making lots of money and copy what he's doing." – J. Paul Getty

William Eckhardt started his career in 1974, which was four years after his doctoral studies experience at the University of Chicago (he failed to finish his studies for a doctoral degree in math). He's published many articles in academic journals. He took part in the Turtle Trading Experiment with Richard Dennis in which he bet against Richard. Richard said the principles used by a guru could be inculcated into trainees, but William didn't think this is possible. At last, some trading principles were inculcated into some novice traders and they later went on to make spectacular results. Thus William was proven wrong.

He founded ETC (Eckhardt Trading Company) in 1991 – a firm which has over $1 billion in trading funds and speculates on great varieties of market instruments. As a result of his strong academic experience, he advocates the use of mathematics and statistics in trading. In a period of 20 years, the ETC made an average of 17.3 per cent per annum (making a record 21.09 per cent in the year 2010). William Eckhardt remains a successful trader and funds manager. More information about ETC can be found at Eckhardttrading.com.

Lessons

I prefer to call William Eckhardt the Oracle of Chicago. Here is the trading insight that comes from the Oracle of Chicago.

1. Incessant transaction activities in the markets ultimately leave some as winners and some as losers. When there's an effective trading principle, that principle would enable only the privileged few to be home and dry. This is a fact that's common in the trading world. Money usually goes from the majority to the minority. The lesson here is that: in order for you to win, you need to adopt the trading principles used by the privileged few. When a trader thinks like an average individual and showcases common emotions, she/he would end up like most people who lose their equity.

2. Successful trading can be taught and it can be learned. This is a truth that William failed to grasp many years ago, but experience showed him otherwise. Now he believes that gifted trading coaches can train people and mentor them until they become experts.

3. In most cases, colossal positivity tend to be more tempting but harmful than colossal negativity, especially when it comes to irrational thinking. It's helpful not to be too happy when there is colossal positivity. People tend to open illogical trades after the markets have smiled on them for a long time. Speaking more on this, William says: "When you're on a big winning streak, there's a temptation to think that you're doing something special, which will allow you to continue to propel yourself upward. You start to think that you can afford to make shoddy decisions. You can imagine what happens next. As a general rule, losses make you strong and profits make you weak."

4. Speculation is like a mirror since people know what they ought not to do; but that's what they do. They know what they ought to do; but that's what they don't do. Winning trading principles go against what most people prefer.

5. Many people believe in cutting their profits before the markets take them. They think they need to quickly take their profits so that the portfolio balances can increase, but this is how many traders end up shooting themselves in the back. When suicide traders sustain large losses because they run their losses, those who call themselves expert make gains that are too insignificant. The trader is her or his own enemy, because of the normal human tendency to anticipate and to dread. When you have a losing trade, you anticipate that it'll soon turn positive; whereas the loss simply becomes bigger (it could have been smaller than that if you'd not anticipated anything). When you have a winning trade, you dread the possibility that it'll soon turn negative, and you take your profit prematurely. The dread has prevented you from riding the market that is about to go in your favour by several hundreds of pips. For you to be a triumphant trader, you need to bring these two counterproductive emotions to subjection. You need to do the exact opposite of what most others will do: when you are

supposed to dread the possibility of a trade going against you, that's the best time to anticipate further profit from that trade. When you are supposed to anticipate that a negative trade could turn positive, that's the best time to dread the possibility of it not turning positive, and therefore resulting in much more unbearable negativity.

Conclusion

The factor behind the markets is this: There are always bulls and bears in the markets, and some of them capitalize on new trading opportunities just before you recognize them. Did you ever wonder whether there are still bulls in an overextended northward bias? Many ignore this probability, including you, for the market continues to move upwards as the buying pressure exists. Yet, how can this be ascertained? You might then want to shift gears and bear it in mind that some experts tend to see new trading opportunities earlier than you. What's the kind of trading mentality possessed by those experts who tend to see trading opportunities before you do and thus capitalize on them; thereby making decent gains?

This article concludes with a quote from William:

"Don't think about what the market's going to do; you have absolutely no control over that. Think about what you're going to do if it gets there. In particular, you should spend no time at all thinking about those rosy scenarios in which the market goes your way, since in those situations, there's nothing more for you to do. Focus instead on those things you want least to happen and on what your response will be."

CHAPTER 12

Thomas Rowe Price:
The Father of Growth Investing

"I never blamed the market... I had to have the proper process from mentality to preparation to execution if I was going to make it." – Anthony Crudele

Thomas Rowe Price, Jr. was born in Maryland, USA. He lived from 1898 to 1983. Receiving his first degree in chemistry (Swarthmore College), he had first-hand experience of the economic Depression, and instead of developing a great hate for the markets, he fell in love with them. Yes, he found that he preferred figures to chemicals. He began working at a brokerage firm in Baltimore, where he worked his way up the company's ladder.

Because he didn't see eye-to-eye with the investment philosophy of the firm he worked for, he established his own firm in 1937 – T. Rowe Price Associates. He invariably gave his investors' interests a priority, also charging investment-based fees rather than commissions. The logic is this: if your investors succeed, you'll succeed too. He founded a mutual fund in 1950, which he presided over till he retired. The Fund, named T. Rowe Price Growth Stock Fund, was actually purchased by his erstwhile workers. Yet it remains a functional trading firm till today.

Lessons

What can we learn from this mad genius?

1. What others see as reasons for abandoning the markets are what trading geniuses see as the reasons for embracing the markets. I've seen misinformed people swearing never to trade or invest again because of the effects of the 2008 bear markets. What happened then has made some traders reach the pinnacle of their achievements. Thomas' early years as a market player made him come to grips with the effects of the Depression, but this only made him a better market player.

2. Customers, clients and investors come first. They need to be given priority in everything. If this is done, then you'll be well compensated. This is what Thomas believed, and it worked for him, just as it still works today.

3. Honestly, the best market forecasters don't know tomorrow with utmost certainty. The art of forecasting is essentially probabilistic in nature. You don't know what'll happen in a few years' time, not to mention several years. There are rivals, cutting-edge innovations, and so on. These things can have severe impact in the world of trading. The only thing you can be sure of is that

there'll always be changes, and the only thing you can always control is your risk.

4. Why was Thomas a successful investor? He knew the markets have some patterns caused by herd mentality. The logic is to go against that herd mentality, not to go with the crowd. His investment approach; which is growth investing, was totally something that looked so novel. It's all about specializing on some instruments that could go northward in the long term. Self-control, sticking to his strategy and good knowledge of the fundamentals are some of his secret principles.

5. Thomas was called the father of growth investing because he believed that hot and well-organized companies can deliver returns that could outpace the growth rate of the economy. Therefore good research is needed in stock picking, diversification, and risk reduction. These principles have proven to be correct. When selecting stocks, Thomas often considered a company's research excellence in product developments, absence of deadly rivals, non-intervention by the government, cost-effective budget, well-compensated workers, decent percentage profit, good profit margin, and an enviable increase in earnings per share. This is the definition of a growth stock. The shares of a company are worth holding as long as this definition is still valid. When it's clear that the definition is no longer valid, it's time to dump the shares. Newbies can use these principles successfully.

6. Thomas was smart enough to know when to hold on to stocks and when to let go. Although he espoused growth investing for more than three decades, he tended to become aware of the blind overconfidence of the public. When the price gains had gone too far and the public enthusiasm was irrational, then the bullish biases were over. He knew when to sell. Do you also have exit strategies?

Conclusion

Rookies tend to visualize how much they can make from the markets, without thinking of how they can control the impact of the uncertainty when things go wrong. You can really control what happens to your account... plus you can deal with your trades with clean rationality. Strategies that make sense have logical positive expectancy incorporated into them, since following the line of the least resistance may sometimes have very low accuracy.

This piece ends with a quote from Thomas:

"It is better to be early than too late in recognizing the passing of one era, the waning of old investment favourites and the advent of a new era affording new opportunities for the investor."

CHAPTER 13

Lee Ainslie:
A Hedge Fund Maverick

"My mood is best when I execute according to my plan regardless of outcome." –
Derek Hernquist

Lee Ainslie III is a trader and a self-made American billionaire who
lives in Dallas, Texas. He's happily married with kids. He got his BA
at the University of Virginia and his MBA at University of North
Carolina. He worked for Julian Robertson at Tiger Management.
Three years later, he began to run Sam Wyly's Maverick Capital,
whose initial fund totalled $38 million. Being a managing partner at
Maverick Capital Ltd (New York and Dallas), Lee is a hedge fund
manager who manages assets that are worth $10 billion. He was
making decent profits when, unfortunately, Tiger Management was

making considerable losses. He's involved in some boards and charities.

Lessons

These are the lessons from Lee, a trading maverick at Maverick capital:

1. Lee's main watchword is integrity. Integrity is crucial in your personal character and business. Talented and experienced partners also help a lot. At the end of everything, the real asset a business can have is people. People tend to perform better when they are inspired and encouraged.

2. Lee has no magic trading systems, yet his strategies work over time. Where many greedy and impatient traders evaluate their results on a daily, weekly, monthly or even quarterly basis, Lee's company evaluates their trading results every few years' time or so. This has allowed great stability, consistency and comfort.

3. Your beliefs about other types of business can't help you in trading. Ironically, the rookie speculators tend to take high risk and think every trading method they are using is foolproof. This emphasizes the real need for coaching and the fact that trying experiences would personally be had by the budding trader. In contrary to what certain traders want, Lee doesn't double his portfolios quickly over short periods of time. On his funds, he makes something like 24%, 11.1%, 33.3%, 45.4%, 17.4% etc. He doesn't go for 100%, 150%, 250% 1,500%, 2,600% etc. You know, that's possible, but too risky. So go for smaller returns, which mean you need to lower your expectations.

4. It isn't safe to think high probability trades are what bring low risk. What really brings low risk is small position sizing and conservative risk control. Targeting 1,500%, 100%, 3,500% and so

on is high risk which comes with very huge drawdowns. When one has an open position, one may feel reluctant to smooth them – particularly when the stake is high and one refuses to change one's opinion and is determined to hold the positions indefinitely. On the other hand, targeting small percentages is low risk. One advantage of low risk is that it comes with minor drawdowns when there's negativity. In the year 2011, Lee's main fund had a roll-down of 14.8%. You know, that roll-down was small enough to be recovered. Despite occasional roll-downs, Lee has always made a comeback. Do you have a positive expectancy strategy? You'll occasionally experience short-term or protracted losses. However, if you stick to that positive expectancy, you'll always make a comeback.

Conclusion

Good trading mentors breed great traders. Lee Ainslie once worked for Julian Robertson (father of hedge funds). Now he's a great trader. No doubt Julian Robertson would be very proud of him. Do you have a good mentor at the moment? Perhaps you can become another great trader, even if your capital is very much smaller.

This chapter concludes with a quote from Lee:

"There are no 'holds.' Every day you're either willing to buy more at the current price, or, if you aren't, you should redeploy the capital to something you believe does deserve incremental capital."

CHAPTER 14

Emilio Tomasini:
Trading with Unusual Sense of Humour

"There's no doubt that the RRR is tremendously important. To get big profits, you have to take minor risks." – Larry Williams

Emilio Tomasini is an Italian Professor of Corporate Finance at University of Bologna, and he's a full time market speculator, trading several financial markets. He founded LombardReport.com, which is a renowned online newspaper for serious investors and traders. He also serves as a consultant to top traders. He's a former columnist at TRADERS'. Now he manages and directs other trading publications. He's still a regular columnist and an author of best-selling books. His articles are full of funny but factual trading ideas. His website is Emiliotomasini.it.

Lessons

Professor Emilio is best understood by visiting his website and reading his past articles. However here are few of the numerous lessons that can be learned from him:

1. You can have fun while trading – real fun. Professor Emilio has an unusual sense of humour which is often evident in his articles. Trading, as a fantastic way of life, is worth enjoying.

2. Traders these days are lucky because they have sophisticated technologies and great trading facilities at their disposal. Many decades ago, these things were not available and the pieces of price data available then were few and far between. Trading conditions were not as favourable as they are today. Nevertheless, successful traders existed in those days. If there were those who succeeded in those days in spite of harsh conditions, why can't you succeed with all the trading facilities and technologies at your disposal? You now have access to real-time data that comes to you at the speed of light. For instance, there are great pieces of trading software out there. One of the most popular among Forex traders is the Meta Trader.

3. Are you a systematic trader or a discretionary trader? Systematic traders hate discretionary trading methods while discretionary traders abhor systematic trading methods. Each camp has certain advantages and disadvantages: both camps can be successful if they control their risk.

4. Talking about the biggest names in the trading world, like David Tepper, Paul Tudor Jones and others, we know it's inspiring and encouraging reading about them and their mindset and trading approaches. However, it also pays if we pay attention to being the best traders we can be. If you concentrate on being the best trader, perhaps you can become a big name in future.

5. Making money is easy, but retaining it is difficult. With the control of the uncertainty in your trading, you can give up as little as possible in your profit, and as such, you'll later recover your profits and move on.

6. One of the major problems in trading is that most traders don't have enough money to invest. That's why we're always under pressure to use aggressive money management so that our small portfolios can double quickly. Do you want to make $100,000 per annum? For a trader who has a capital of $1 million, that's pretty possible because he only has to make 10% returns per annum. But someone whose capital is only $5,000 would need to make about 2,000% before she/he can go home with $100,000 per annum. Can you see why some find trading difficult?

7. The bigger the lot sizes you use, the bigger your profits when there is positivity, but the bigger the roll-downs when there is negativity. Since we're not absolutely sure of what the next candle would be, a charting technique that gives some readings in a bear market may have completely different readings in a bull market. The greatest risk control can't force a negative position to turn to positivity when the market has not moved determinedly in your favour. When your lot sizes aren't too big and you're conservative about your risk, you'll eventually be paid by the markets.

Conclusion

One mentor once told me this: "If it's not painful, it can't be gainful." How true is this statement in trading and in other spheres of human endeavours?

I'd like to conclude this chapter with a quote from Professor Emilio:

"A good money management can improve the results of your trading system. So you need not have a superb trading system to make money. In the long term, it's enough to have a stable strategy with positive expectancy and a proper money management."

CHAPTER 15

James Simons:
How Did He Become a
Global Legendary Trader?

"It took me many years of study to learn my trade as a biochemist, so why did I think I could master trading in a few weeks?" – Lee Bohl

James Harry Simons (sometimes known as Jim Simons) is a great American funds manager, philanthropist and mathematician. He was born in 1938 and raised in Massachusetts. He got his BSc in math at the age of 20 and his PhD in math at the age of 23. He was a member of research staff at IDA (Institute for Defense Analyses) from 1964 to 1968. He also taught math at Harvard. He chaired the math department at Stony Brook University in 1968. He was the recipient of American Mathematical Society's Oswald Veblen Prize in Geometry, in 1976.

In 1978, James left the academic world to manage a fund – using a discretionary approach. Since then, he's been successful. He ultimately founded Renaissance Technologies, a private investment portfolio, in 1982. The portfolio was worth over $15 billion. His fund became one of the most profitable funds in the world. In the year 2004, he earned $670 million. He made an income of $1.7 billion in the year 2006, plus $1.5 billion in the year 2005. In the year 2007, he made an additional $2.5 billion as an income. He's therefore one of the highest paid funds managers in the world. Being worth $10.6 billion, he's declared as the seventy-fourth wealthiest individual on earth (twenty-seventh position in the USA). James retired in 2009 as CEO of Renaissance Technologies. He lives in New York with his wife. He fathered five children: one drowned at the age 24 of in Indonesia, and another was killed in an automobile accident. The remaining three are alive. He has several grandkids.

Lessons

Here are some of the lessons that can be learned from this world trading legend:

1. James' fund uses algorithm/math models to make trading decisions and open positions. These computer-based models analyse data and prognosticate future prices in the markets, with a high degree of success. Contrary to what some experts think, automated trading works, and it can work with permanent success, just like manual trading. What makes robots fail is the fact that their makers program worse expectancy rules into them. If programmers put positive expectancy rules into trading robots, they'll be victorious in the long-term, just like their human counterparts. Unfortunately, this is contrary to what most trading

robot makers prefer (since the majority of them aren't expert traders).

2. Renaissance Technologies hires many experts who are not traders. These include experts in math, statistics and physics. Their strong academic know-how is capitalized on in the trading world. While success in trading requires some things different than what most other professions require, great professionals in other fields can make a huge difference in the trading world if they are groomed to approach the markets in the right way. It's not uncommon to see great traders who are extant or former psychologists, engineers, politicians, businessmen, programmers, doctors, lecturers, sportsmen, astronauts, etc. Have you mastered an area of human endeavour which can be used to your advantage if blended with the correct trading principles? As of James, one professor of physics says it's stupefying to see a math expert achieving enviable goals in trading. Some people also wonder how that can be feasible. Yes, this is feasible. When you become a constantly successful trader, some would wonder how you manage to do that.

3. James was a victim of Bernard Madoff's Ponzi scheme. Innocently, he even recommended that the Stony Brook University Foundation invest with Madoff, when he was chairman of that Foundation. The Foundation lost $5.4 million as a result of this. There's no one that can't be scammed. Scammers are too smart; even for learned people.

4. James is a great philanthropist: he's a benefactor of many charity and educational programs in the US and overseas. He co-founded Paul Simons Foundation so that education and health projects can be supported. He donates larger amounts of money to support Nepalese healthcare. This is done through Nick Simons Institute (to commemorate his son, Nick, who drowned in Indonesia). He

founded Math for America, a non-profit organization which seeks to improve math education in public schools. He helped raise $13 million to prevent the shutdown of the Relativistic Heavy Ion Collider because of pecuniary shortage. He gave $25 million to Stony Brook University to benefit its math and physics departments. He later gave another $150 million to Stony Brook University. Through the Simons Foundation, he gave $60 million to start the Simons Center for Geometry and Physics at Stony Brook. He gave $60 million to start the Simons Institute for the Theory of Computing at UC Berkeley. When you become highly successful financially, please think of those you can help. There are more blessings in giving than in receiving.

Conclusion

James' career and financial success is really enviable, but it didn't come without effort. For you to enjoy success in trading, you need to put in more effort. Success is inspiration plus perspiration. Don't rest on your laurels; if you want to enjoy the rewards, you will have to endure the efforts.

This piece ends with a quote from Emilio Tomasini, a onetime TRADERS' columnist (concerning James):

"Maybe you know the name of Jim Simons, that biggest algorithm trader who manages a fund whose name is Magellan, and that he made a cumulative composite yearly return of 40% over the last 15 years. And he became a world legend." (Source: www.traders-mag.com)

CHAPTER 16

William O'Neil:
Outperforming the Markets

"We want to generate sustainable returns where nobody needs to have a guilty conscience." – Norbert Lohrke

William J. O'Neil was born on 25 March 1933, in Oklahoma City. He grew up in Texas. In Dallas, Texas, he attended Woodrow Wilson High School. After he got his first degree in business from Southern Methodist University, he joined the USAF (the United States Air Force). He later joined a brokerage firm and began to develop some trading methods. William has been influenced by many bright trading minds, including Gerald Loeb and Nicolas Darvas. In 1960, he attended Harvard Business School in order to study Management Development.

At the age of 30, he acquired a seat on the New York Stock Exchange (being the youngest person to do so at that time). In 1963, he started William O'Neil + Co. Incorporated. The company made some innovative contributions to the trading world – something that's still relevant to more than 10,000 companies. He created Daily Graphs in 1972 and founded O'Neil Data Systems, Inc. in 1973. In 1984, he started Investor's Daily, which has proven to be a formidable rival to The Wall Street Journal. He launched MarketSmith, an online shares research tool, in 2010. He wrote a number of books, some of which are *How To Make Money In Stocks* (1988), *24 Essential Lessons For Investment Success* (1999) and *The Successful Investor* (2003). He has won certain awards in various fields. His official website is: Williamoneil.com.

Lessons

Here are some simple but weighty lessons that can be learned from William O'Neil:

1. William invented the renowned CAN SLIM strategy; which has enabled him to become the best-performing trader in his company. This strategy incorporates fundamental and chart-based trading approaches, with the selection of the stocks that are the most promising. If you're interested in CAN SLIM and how it helps in trading, you'd need to study it. If you have a great strategy already, congrats! You'll just need to stick to it.

2. The markets have a knack for going against the expectation of the public, and because of this, what most analysts are saying can't be relied on. Most analysts tend to mislead the public by trying to drive home their hypotheses, which aren't always accurate. Expert and personal forecasts can't enable you to outperform the markets constantly. What'll eventually help you are the markets and the realities on them.

3. It's common for some people to call long trades because they think a market is oversold, but in most cases the market would trend further southward. The same is true of a bull market: when people think it's overbought and should experience a protracted pullback, then it would rally further. This means that one should trade what one sees, and doesn't need to trade against the trend.

4. It's appalling that some traders tend to talk of how much they can make in a day or in a month (in terms of pips, points or base currency). They tend to ignore the fact that the only thing they can control is how much they lose. Just focus on losing as little as possible: that's the secret to your outperforming the markets.

Conclusion

Blessed is he/she who considers risk and takes appropriate measures to curtail it. People risk too much because of overconfidence, which has brought many potential gurus' dreams to an abrupt end. Then, it pays to be realistic when trading, so that one remains emotionless while speculating. Between 40% and 50% of one's trades can end up in the negative territory, based on the price conditions. You'd do well to merely close your negative positions and look forward to other opportunities in the markets. Trading will offer you with many great signals, and as such, your new trades may recover the losses you have sustained. You may refuse to be a failure in spite of the disappointment that comes occasionally.

This piece ends with a quote from William:

"The whole secret to winning and losing in the stock market is to lose the least amount possible when you're not right."

CHAPTER 17

Nicolas Darvas:
His Timeless Trading Strategy

"I knew now that I had to keep rigidly to the system I had carved out for myself."
– Nicolas

Born in 1920, in Hungary, Nicolas Darvas was a popular dancer, self-educated trader and an accomplished author. He was a good economist at the University of Budapest. During World War II, he didn't want to stay in Hungary until the country was overrun by either the Nazi military or the Soviet military, so he improvised a travelling document in 1943 (at the age of 23) and fled the country. While in Turkey, he was able to avoid dying of hunger because he had 50 GBP with him. Later he came across his half-sister Julia. Julia then became his dancing team member. His troupe later became renowned globally, with outstanding achievements in Europe and the United States.

During his leisure times, he read many trading and investment books, some of which are *ABC of Investing* by R. C. Effinger, *Consistent Profits In The Stock Market* by Curtis Dahl, *Profit In The Stock Market* by H. M. Gartley, *The Battle for Investment Survival* by Gerald M. Loeb (1935) among others. When he invested in some over-extended bull markets, the markets continue to go northward and thus were able to give him nice profits. Thus he was able to create the strategy that made him famous. With the strategy, he turned $36,000 into more than $2.25 million in a 36-month period. While travelling with his troupe, he'd check Barron's magazine, see what the markets were doing, and send cable/telegram messages to his broker in New York, so that new trades could be executed in his behalf. He made use of the latest technology of his days.

Which strategy did Nicolas use to tackle the uncertainty of the markets? His strategy was based on the popular Box Theory. With this kind of theory, certain price actions were seen as a series of boxes. Whenever the price was in a box, he stayed out of the market. But once the price broke out northward from inside the box, he went long, setting a stop according to his rule. Nicolas himself explains in details how he used that strategy in his book titled: *How I Made 2,000,000 in the Stock Market* (1960). His other books are *Wall Street: The Other Las Vegas* (1964), *The Anatomy of Success* (1965), *The Darvas System for Over-The-Counter Profits* (1971) and *You Can Still Make It in the Market* (1977).

He died in 1977, at the age of 57.

Lessons

What lessons can be learned from this famous dancer, author and trader? Here are some of them:

1. A normal market must be a two-way market (a market in which you can either go long or short). Go long in a bull market and go short in a bear market and do it right. Nicolas Darvas was a permabull, for short-selling didn't fit his mindset, but he acknowledged that his Box Theory could be used conversely for taking advantage of bear markets. Bear markets offer fast profit-making opportunities and savvy speculators ought to consider this fact. Don't buy in bear markets; otherwise, stay out of the markets.

2. If you're a successful trader, the psychological principles that enable you to trade successfully can also be used to achieve your goals in other business. There are market wizards who are also successful academicians, businessmen, programmers, sportsmen, etc. There are people like James Simons and William O'Neil out there. Nicolas believed that the formula for success remains essentially the same.

3. Nicolas invested in shares of companies that had good growth potential, like electronics and missile industries in his days. He called himself a techno-fundamental trader, which means that a combination of technical and fundamental analysis is good.

4. You see, strategies that work will continue to work irrespective of how old they are. Nicolas' Box method still works perfectly in today's markets. Whenever he saw a signal, he quickly sent orders for trades to be opened. Like many traders today, he didn't hesitate, for he knew that the trend is the trader's buddy. Many traders today would be reluctant to open trades because they know too much (often conflicting ideas). The problem most of us face right now is the availability of too much knowledge. Nicolas bought mainly because the he saw bullish signals on his chart, and in reality, whatever worked effectively in the past may also be effective in the future. The Box Theory was created over fifty

years ago, yet it still works. This is because the Theory showcases the speculators' mindset and weaknesses. Yes, old legendary trading strategies can still work if they are stuck to faithfully.

5. There are entry and exit plans in every trading system. If studied very well, it can be seen that the Box method has entry and exit plans. The best exit method in any system is the stop loss. Nicolas decided to let his stop loss decide when to exit in a bull market.

6. Analysis is good, but it doesn't predict the market. So there's a big difference between analysis and market prediction. This must be borne in mind. Like technical analysis, all that fundamental analysis can let you know are the facts of yesterday and today, not what must happen tomorrow.

7. Don't be overconfident in the market, no matter how good your trading system is or how favourably the markets have treated you. Overconfidence is definitely not a good thing. Nicolas said that's the most harmful mindset that can be developed by any trader.

Conclusion

Your trading career would bring out the best and the worst in you; therefore you'd do well to come to terms with your strong and weak points before you stake your neck. This would enable you to do things that could bring out the best in you and avoid things that could bring the worst in you. With this method, you'll be able to render your weak points ineffectual, so that they don't have any adverse effects on your trading.

This piece ends with another quote from Nicolas:

"I was successful in taking larger profits than losses in proportion to the amounts invested."

CHAPTER 18

Mellody Hobson:
A Leader in the World of Investing

"To ignore the facts of what you see in the market does not change the facts." –
Old Trader

Mellody Hobson was born on 3 April 1969 in Chicago, Illinois. She's an American investor, trader and businesswoman. She got her BA from Princeton's Woodrow Wilson School of Public and International Affairs. In addition, she has bagged honorary PhDs from St. Mary's College and Howard University.

After receiving her BA, she started working at Ariel Investments, LLC. She began to climb the ladder of success within that company: from being an intern to being a senior V.P. and Director of

Marketing. Finally, she became the firm's president. This firm, based in Chicago, is one of the largest Afro-American-owned mutual funds and funds management firms in the USA, with over $3 billion in assets. Mellody is the Chair of the Board of Trustees of Ariel Mutual Funds and Dreamworks Animation SKG, Inc. She's spread her tentacles into businesses, programs and foundations. She's been featured in many popular magazines, along with extraordinary achievers like herself. Her corporate website is: Arielinvestments.com.

In the year 2006, she started dating billionaire George Walton Lucas, Jr., American businessman, movie producer and screenwriter. They got married on 22 June 2013.

Lessons

Here are some of the lessons that can be learned from this illustrious black American:

1. As it's been said somewhere else, successful trading and investing has nothing to do with one's colour, race, education background, religion, class, gender, country of origin and other discriminatory factors. Consistent survival in financial markets has no borders and can be attained by you.

2. On the official website of Ariel Investment, there's something there that piques my interest. There's a saying there that goes thus: "Slow and steady wins the race." How important and timeless this trading truth is! Contrary to those who think they can double their account many times in a month or in a quarter or in a year, investing and speculation strategies that work entail very slow, but steady equity increase. In trading, those who sprint too fast like the hare or the horse are bound to crash at last. Trading is an activity that makes us get rich slowly, not quickly. I'll be happy with 15% profit per annum if my capital is safe. Or what's the

sense in targeting hundreds of percentage of returns per annum while your capital vanishes after a margin call? The tortoise and the snail move slowly, but if you go to sleep, they'll have moved far by the time you wake up. What initially looks like a very slow movement translates into a great distance over a long period of the time.

3. Mellody advises people that they should forget fear. Many people hate or are afraid to invest their money in the markets because they think they can lose it. When the markets crash and become too undervalued, that's when most people would be afraid to buy (and that's the best time to buy). When the markets rise and rise significantly over a long period of the time, thus becoming very expensive, that's when most people would want to buy (and that's the best time to sell). When the market is overbought, people have no fear (and that's when they should be fearful). When the market is oversold, people are fearful (and that's when they should be confident). As you can see, people's investment timing is invariably wrong. They buy when they should be selling and they sell when they should be buying. It's a pity that people don't want to sell for profits when the markets are overvalued and dear. Rather, they sell for loss when the markets are undervalued and very cheap. That is the opposite of what you should be doing in the markets.

Conclusion

In one of his past newsletters, Joe Ross (Tradingeducators.com) said that there's an old adage which goes thus: "It is better to have loved and lost than to have never loved at all." Joe then continued that similarly, anyone who desires pecuniary freedom had better make attempts and lose money during the initial futile attempts, than to stay in a state of complacency and merely wish he'd made an attempt. Such a person could spend the rest of her/his life feeling bad because he'd failed to utilize the opportunities of a lifetime, for the person would perceive the fact that if she/he had taken steps the dreams could've been actualized.

This piece ends with a quote from Mellody:

"I know many members of our community steer clear of Wall Street because of the perception that the stock market is risky, but I am convinced the biggest risk of all is not taking one."

CHAPTER 19

Richard Donchian:
The Father of Trend Following

"In the end, by becoming astutely aware of what can go wrong, and taking control, we can maintain our winning edge." – Joe Ross

Richard Donchian, who was an American trader and pioneer of managed futures, lived from 1905 until 1993. His parents were Armenians who came to settle in the US. Richard graduated from Yale, earning a BA in Economics. He started showing interest in stock markets after he read a book about Jesse Livermore (Reminiscences of a Stock Operator). Though he lost some money in the significant bear markets that occurred in the year 1929, he simply used the experience to focus more on chart analysis, paying attention to price actions.

In 1930, he began to deal with Wall Street. He produced a renowned service called Security Pilot and sold it to brokers. He then worked in various capacities at Hemphill, Noyes and Co and Samuel Rug Company. During World War II, he joined the American army, even getting promoted in USAF. When the War was over, he returned to trading, working again in various capacities until he founded Futures, Inc. which was one of the earliest publicly traded commodity portfolios.

Richard started a rule-based trading methodology which was later called Trend Following. He believed that markets trended according to their biases for a considerable period of the time. He used moving averages and published various articles on his trading approaches. Thus he came to be known as the father of trend following. In 1960, he was chosen as director of Commodity Research with Hayden Stone, and he started writing a trading newsletter that focused on commodity trend timing. In his lifetime, he was a member of various exchanges.

Richard was a successful trader: he died as a soldier on the battlefield of the financial markets. He was able to turn $0.2 million into $18 million over many years (though this wasn't easy at all, for he faced drawdowns along the way). Many modern trend-following strategies, including the Turtle trading system, are based on his original ideas. The Richard Davoud Donchian Foundation – a charity organization – was founded in his honour.

Lessons

While alive, Richard published a set of principles that could help today's traders:

1. Effective trading strategies have to come with rational approaches to money management. Richard dedicated himself to conservative trade management rules, and today's traders can also achieve success by being conservative as well.

2. Widespread public opinions tend to be wrong. Even when they are right, it pays to dither before one takes decisions on the markets.

3. Following equilibrium phases in the markets, you would do well to follow the direction of protracted movements when breakouts occur.

4. No matter what your trading rules are, you need to curtail your negative trades and allow your positive trades to make more gains.

5. Richard had trading guidelines that acted as filters (which can't be mentioned here). There ought to be rational filters in your speculation guidelines. For example, one needs to know when to risk more and when to risk less while trading.

6. Go long in bullish markets and go short in bearish markets; though this rule is dependent on other factors.

Conclusion

In the midst of our daily concerns about risk, negative trades, and how to make profits, we may lose sight of the most important aspect of trading. When successful in the markets, we too may also forget our limitations and allow our hearts to be filled with dangerous overconfidence. On a different note, we may find ourselves lamenting moments in trading that don't go our way, rather than focusing on the moments that do go our way.

This chapter concludes with a quote from Richard:

"Nobody has ever been able to demonstrate that a complex mathematical equation can answer the question: Is the market moving in an uptrend, downtrend or simply just sideways?"

CHAPTER 20

Charlie Munger:
A Replica of Warren Buffett

"True success is the only thing that you cannot have unless and until you have offered it to others."

Charles Thomas Munger was born on 1 January 1924, in Omaha, Nebraska, USA (Warren Buffet is also a native of Omaha). He's a lawyer, business mogul, Philanthropist and investor. He studied math at the University of Michigan and served in the U.S. Army Air Corps. Then he was admitted to study law at Harvard. In 1948, he settled in California and started practicing law. In 1962, he worked as a real estate lawyer. Later, he stopped practicing law and focused on investment management. As a result of this, he collaborated with Otis Booth and later, Jack Wheeler, to found Wheeler, Munger, &

Co. It was an investment company which had a seat on the Pacific Coast Stock Exchange. From 1962 to 1975, the partnership made compound annual profits of roughly 20%. After about 31% in 1976, the company was folded up.

Charles is best known for his work with Buffett (the latter calls him his partner). He formerly chaired Wesco Financial Corporation, which is now part of Berkshire Hathaway. At the time of writing this article, Charles is Vice-chairman of Berkshire Hathaway Corporation. He's also the chairman of the Daily Journal Corporation. His net worth is $1.1 billion. As a philanthropist, he's donated hundreds of millions of dollars to schools (including universities). He's been married twice, having six children altogether.

Lessons

These are some of the lessons you can learn from Charles:

1. His investment partnership made some compounded annual profits of roughly 20% between 1962 and 1975. When there were losses of up to 31% in the year 1976, the partnership was ended. Nevertheless, he didn't quit the investment world (contrary to what most people do today whenever there's a significant negativity in their investment, without thinking of the days when things were going their way). He simply moved ahead in another format and has been astoundingly successful since then.

2. Do you work with someone who differs from you in certain ways? Your differences shouldn't cause a rift. Instead, you should focus on your partner's admirable qualities. In spite of political, operational and interest differences, Charles has been working wonderfully together with Warren Buffett.

3. Charles donated millions of dollars to education. He still donates more and more money. Some might be concerned about his net

worth being drastically reduced, but he said he'll not need the money where he's going. He's now close to 90 years of age: do you think he'll need the money in his grave? Even if he was the richest man in the world, would that matter to him in his grave?

4. According to Charles, a number of selected stocks that have been studied and mastered can generate excellent profits in the long run. A good trading strategy can give you average profits that are much bigger than average losses over time.

5. People perform well when they are encouraged and motivated. In a workplace, high ethical standards are needed. Charles once said that good businesses are those with ethics. No business can thrive long on trickery and shenanigans.

6. The more you stay in trading, the more expertise you gain. More years means more wisdom. Besides, for you to master a broad subject matter area, you need to read all the time. For you to master the art of trading, you need to read more and more about it.

7. A simple idea can be all you need to get your long-awaited breakthrough. Simple strategy ideas can be all you need to become a permanently successful trader. Take simple ideas seriously. Charles said that it never ceases to amaze him how much territory can be grasped if one merely masters and consistently uses all the obvious and easily learned principles.

8. For you to succeed in trading you don't have to be brilliant: you just need to be a little wiser than other traders, on average, for a long period of time.

9. Teaching people to master what they don't know initially is a great thing. Being an effective trading coach is a great calling.

10. Charles says he tries to get rid of people who always confidently answer questions about which they don't have any real knowledge.

Conclusion

Actually, judge the current level of your expertise in trading. Would you hire someone to manage your money if he'd acquired only the level of your expertise? Would you recommend such a one to trade for an investment bank? I know you'd not do that, for it would end up ruining a big amount of your portfolio. Doesn't that then show a need for you to obtain more knowledge? You think you're a smart trader, but you still exhibit some rookie's reactions when it comes to the outcome of your trades. You'd need to know the type of trader you are so that you can learn a lot from what happens to you. Oftentimes, you simply need to go through some trying, harrowing and disturbing experiences before you can attain your goal of trading mastery. This is what has happened to many who have mastered the markets.

This chapter concludes with a quote from Charles:

"All intelligent investing is value investing — acquiring more than you are paying for... You're looking for a mispriced gamble. That's what investing is. And you have to know enough to know whether the gamble is mispriced. That's value investing."

CONCLUSION

Trading remains one of the best ways to financial freedom. You can become a great trader. Great traders have no ideas where the markets would be in seven days' time (not to mention a year's time), yet they use that uncertainty to their advantage and stick to their winning trading plans. Market wizards are used to the unpredictability of the markets. They know they will be wrong sometimes; which is a fact, and they are still permanently victorious. According to Dr. Van K. Tharp, one of the best trading coaches in the world, dealing with the market has many such up and down periods. In order to profit from the up periods, you have to tolerate or even "enjoy" the down periods. "In order to enjoy the profits, you have to go through losses... loss has nothing to do with being right or wrong..."

Whatever has happened to you in the markets, whether you won or lost a trade, a brighter future awaits you. Your winnings are evidence that you are making progress: your losses are also a unique opportunity for you to learn from your mistakes and become a better trader. All people who are now billionaires in the markets made mistakes in the past, and they turned the mistakes into valuable assets that made them go ahead. Whatever happened to you, it could have been better or it could have been worse. A loss is a temporary defeat and a blessing in disguise. Falling down is not a defeat, staying down is.

No matter what your trading results have been in the past, trading remains one of the best ways to the ultimate attainment of financial freedom. During the recent global credit crunch, many people became fearful of the future, because economic crises sometimes compel good organizations to dismiss their responsible workers. Many people did not realize this until it happened to them. They thought they only needed to work hard, and their job would be secure, and they would enjoy the ensuing financial security. But after the myth has been busted, many people became so anxious about a poor financial future and the effects it could have on their family. Then many people started seeing trading as a great option: you can trade successfully anywhere, as long as you have access to a good internet connection and then enjoy financial security. The riches inherent in the markets are limitless, though it would be realistic to walk towards this gradually. Please renew your determination and partake in the journey to financial freedom.

You can trade successfully!

ABOUT THE AUTHOR

Azeez Mustapha is a trading professional, funds manager, an InstaForex official analyst, a blogger at ADVFN.com, and a freelance author for trading magazines. He works as a trading signals provider at various websites and his numerous articles are posted on many websites such as www.ituglobalforex.blogspot.com.

Contact: azeez.mustapha@analytics.instaforex.com.

MORE BOOKS FROM ADVFN

EVERYTHING YOU NEED TO KNOW ABOUT MAKING SERIOUS MONEY TRADING THE FINANCIAL MARKETS

by Simon Watkins

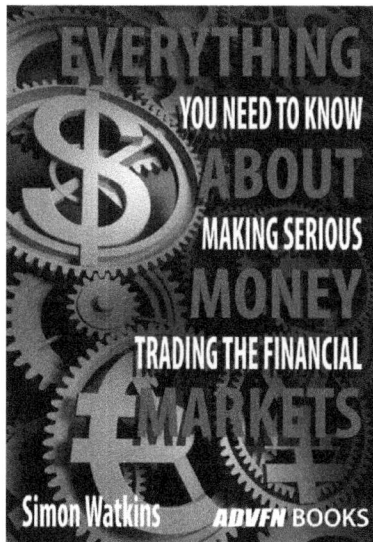

All over the world, people are trading on the financial markets. Some of them make a fortune – and many more lose their shirts. This book tells you how to be one of the winners.

It's a stark and sobering fact that around 90% of retail traders lose all of their trading money within about 90 days. That's because they have little grasp of the realities, technicalities, psychology and nature of the financial markets. In short, they don't know what they are doing.

Everything You Need To Know About Making Serious Money Trading The Financial Markets teaches you how to avoid being one of the 90%, and explains how to stack the odds firmly in your favour so you can become one of the 10% that make life-changing money trading. It's a trading bible that covers all aspects of the subject, from the psychology of trading and the mindset you need to succeed, through the fundamental principles that should guide your trades, to the trading methodologies that will help you succeed.

Fully illustrated with detailed charts, the book shows how you can use technical analysis to make your decisions, how to manage your risk and how to take out hedge positions to offset possible losses.

101 CHARTS FOR TRADING SUCCESS

by Zak Mir

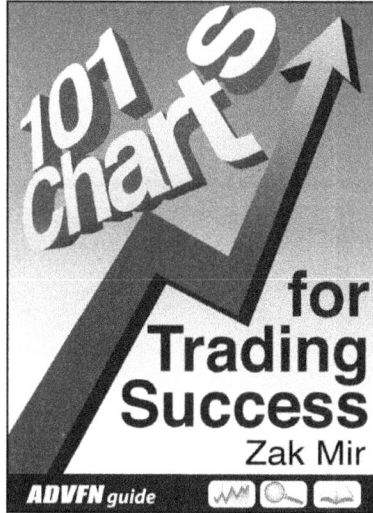

Using insider knowledge to reveal the tricks of the trade, Zak Mir's *101 Charts for Trading Success* explains the most complex set ups in the stock market.

Providing a clear way of predicting price action, charting is a way of making money by delivering high probability percentage trades, whilst removing the need to trawl through company accounts and financial ratios.

Illustrated with easy to understand charts this is the accessible, essential guide on how to read, understand and use charts, to buy and sell stocks. *101 Charts* is a must for all future investment millionaires.

THE GAME
IN WALL STREET

by Hoyle and Clem Chambers

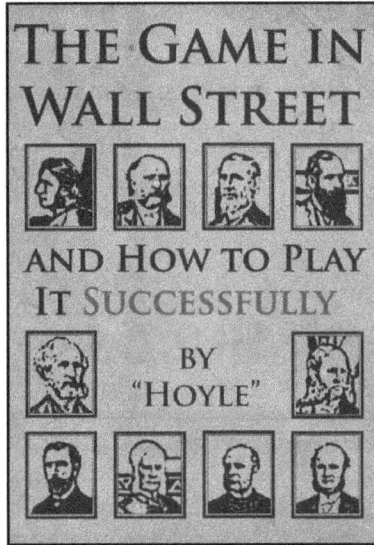

As the new century dawned, Wall Street was a game and the stock market was fixed. Ordinary investors were fleeced by big institutions that manipulated the markets to their own advantage and they had no comeback.

The Game in Wall Street shows the ways that the titans of rampant capitalism operated to make money from any source they could control. Their accumulated funds gave the titans enormous power over the market and allowed them to ensure they won the game.

Traders joining the game without knowing the rules are on a road to ruin. It's like gambling without knowing the rules and with no idea of the odds.

The Game in Wall Street sets out in detail exactly how this market manipulation works and shows how to ride the price movements and make a profit.

And guess what? The rules of the game haven't changed since the book was first published in 1898. You can apply the same strategies in your own investing and avoid losing your shirt by gambling against the professionals.

Illustrated with the very first stock charts ever published, the book contains a new preface and a conclusion by stock market guru Clem Chambers which put the text in the context of how Wall Street operates today.

THE DEATH OF WEALTH

by Clem Chambers

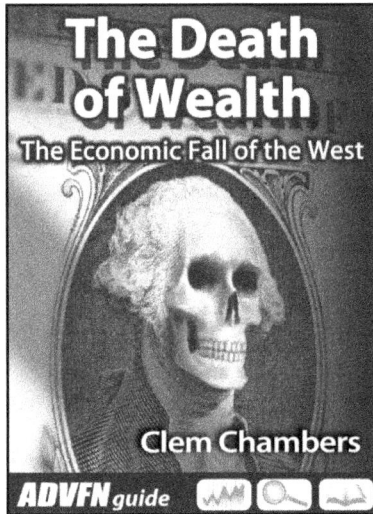

Question: what is the next economic game changer?
Answer: The Death of Wealth.

Market guru Clem Chambers dissects the global economy and the state of the financial markets and lays out the evidence for the death of wealth.

The Death of Wealth flags up the milestones on the route towards impending financial disaster. From the first tentative signs of recovery in the UK and US stock markets at the start of 2012, to the temporary drawing back from the edge of the Fiscal Cliff at the end, the book chronicles the trials and tribulations of the markets throughout the year.

Collecting together articles and essays throughout the last twelve months along with extensive new analysis for 2013, *The Death of*

Wealth allows us to look at these tumultuous events collectively and draw a strong conclusion about what the future holds.

2012 started with the US economy showing signs of recovery, and European financial markets recovering some of the ground lost during the euro crisis. It ended with Obama's re-election and the deal that delayed the plunge off the fiscal cliff by a few months.

In between, the eurozone crisis continued, but none of the affected countries actually left the eurozone; quantitative easing tried to turn things around with the consequences of these "unorthodox" actions yet unknown; and the equity markets after the mid-year correction became strongly bullish.

The Death of Wealth takes you through the events of 2012 month by month, with charts showing the movements of the FTSE 100, the NASDAQ COMPX and the SSE COMPX throughout the year.

With an introduction by renowned market commentator and stock tipster Tom Winnifrith and a summary by trading technical analyst Zak Mir, this collection chronicles the rocky road trip the financial systems of the world have been on and predicts the ultimate destination: the death of wealth as we know it.

www.ingramcontent.com/pod-product-compliance
Lightning Source LLC
Chambersburg PA
CBHW060630210326
41520CB00010B/1546